thousand years of English architecture, if you include the church and castle which are outside the scope of this booklet, but both are treasure houses of history and should be seen as part of the whole. Boroughgate literally means 'town street'.

To return to the borough of Appleby, what we now see is a modification of the original land divisions. Boroughgate had around sixty burgage plots, about thirty on each side. Each plot would therefore have been about 13 yards or twelve metres wide, (information from Martin Holdgate's excellent book on Appleby's history. See 'Further reading.') The street once ran further up the hill beyond the present castle gates and more burgage plots were added in Bridge Street, Doomgate and elsewhere. But the site was cramped, hemmed in by the river. Usually in boroughs, each plot had a **street frontage**, with a **house site (the toft)** behind which lay a **croft**, or long garden area, which terminated in a **back lane**.

On the west side, the back lane is represented by the present Doomgate and Chapel Street but the east side presents the problem of the river. No space was left for a back lane. Instead, each plot ran down to the river bank. Appleby borough as a new town, was a place of merchants and craftsmen, without the agricultural fields and commons which surround many towns.

Appleby market place with horses, carts, covered wagon & thached buildings where post office now stands.

The gardens provided fresh produce and a place for domestic livestock. Horses were of course, until the introduction of first the railways, then the internal combustion engine, the main form of transport for goods and people who could afford them. Chains of pack ponies and riding horses preceded wheeled vehicles, as road surfaces were improved. These animals needed housing and feeding. Evidence of horses and horse-drawn vehicles can be seen in the buildings there today.

Over time, some crofts behind properties have been filled with buildings – stables, dairies, workshops, and other outbuildings. Also, because of the restrictions on expansion placed on the site by the river, cottages and houses have filled up the spaces.

Early photographs show the streets of Appleby with roads before tarmac, which must have become quagmires in wet periods, especially when trampled by hooves of horses and cattle on market days. Market and fair days would have seen the street thronged with traders and customers. Each commodity was allocated an area for trading. The lower part of the market place, between the Moot Hall and High Wiend, was the shambles, the place of butchers and meat traders. Until 1812, when a bull broke loose and caused havoc in the town, bulls were baited before slaughter, as it was believed that made the meat more tender. The bull ring is now in the Information Centre.

Strict rules applied to trading. Selling at reduced prices before the market bell was rung (forestalling) incurred a fine. Weights and volumes of produce had to conform to official measures: short measure was a punishable offence, as was the sale of stale bread, rancid butter, tainted meat or watered-down liquor.

Typical detail of wrought iron fences to front gardens of the west side of Boroughgate.

Markets and fairs were highly profitable enterprises for the owners of market rights, both from charges made to traders (tolls) and fines. A royal charter enabled owners of fair and markets to charge tolls and see off competitors. Appleby borough had such rights by virtue of charters saying that its burgesses could do the same as the burgesses of York. Appleby received twelve charters between 1179 and 1885.

The borough was not ruled over by the lord of the castle, and the rights of the burgesses, or holders of burgages, were jealously guarded. The mayor and corporation ran the town, although a 'fee farm rent' (revenue due to the Crown) had to be paid.

All the buildings seen today have predecessors on the same spot. Successive rebuildings took place over the centuries. No building survives from the medieval period, but archaeologists have investigated many sites and found medieval material – pottery fragments, bones and various other items. Before the great rebuilding phase of the eighteenth century, the scene would have been one of timber and thatch. The repeated destruction of the town by the Scots before the Union of the Crowns in 1603, meant that the less durable buildings could more easily catch fire and be reduced to rubble. In periods of plague, both in livestock and humans, empty buildings would soon deteriorate and become ruinous.

Surviving buildings represent fashion over the past six hundred years or so, the majority being from the eighteenth, nineteenth and early twentieth centuries. Buildings have been adapted and modified to suit the needs of the age, and we are left with a great many features which tell of a past way of life, for instance, the era of horse traffic has left its mark in the numerous carriage archways into back yards, and the age when larger houses had several servants can be deduced from the area steps down to basement entrances. The chimneys clustered on stone stacks, denoted the number of fireplaces which had to be serviced – ashes removed, coal carried up staircases, flues cleaned – many of which have been blocked up with the advent of central heating. And before running water was installed in houses, maids had to carry heavy jugs of water upstairs, and slops down. Until 1874, people had to rely on either their own or public wells for fresh water, when mains were laid. It was even later, in 1882, that a scheme was carried out, to replace the open sewers which ran along streets.

The Boroughgate of today has undergone many changes which have made the lives of residents and visitors so agreeable, but it remains the 'town street', its layout and purpose enduring for a thousand years.

Buildings of Boroughgate

The Cloisters

These form the gateway into St Lawrence's churchyard, and a path which leads to the south entrance to the church, serving the same purpose as a lych gate in country churchyards – a covered area where wedding processions, funerals and other gatherings can assemble. They also offer shelter from the elements and seating for the public. Rebuilt in 1811 to a design by the nationally known architect, Sir Robert Smirke, the building consists of seven Gothic arches, topped by battlements, with the date and arms in the centre. At each end is a two-storey square tower, also battlemented. Shops now occupy the towers and two arches on either side. From here, Boroughgate can be seen in its entirety.

The Cloisters,
Gateway to St. Lawrence's Church.

Low Cross

It is likely that there has been a structure at the north end of the market place since medieval times. The present distinguished pillar was erected in the late seventeenth century, paid for by money bequeathed by the remarkable Lady Anne Clifford, who during her life had restored Appleby Castle and the churches of St Michael and of St Lawrence, where she and her mother are buried. It was rebuilt in 1817 and has been repainted several times, most recently in 2021. The plain column, standing on a square plinth and base of steps, is topped by a cube of stone with sundials on the east, south and west faces, very much resembling those on the Countess's Pillar, near Brougham, erected in 1653 by Lady Anne Clifford. Right on the top is a weather vane.

Crown and Cushion Inn

One of Appleby's inns which were once numerous. Inns not only provided refreshment and accommodation for travellers, but many other services. News was proclaimed and exchanged; newspapers were read by many people; meetings were held (e.g. by Turnpike Trusts); carriers' carts provided regular transport from inns; and stabling for travellers' horses. The Crown and Cushion stands on a prominent corner formed by Low Wiend and Boroughgate, and is at least three hundred years old and probably older. Traces of cruck construction have been found in re-used timber. As it stands, the building has an early eighteenth century door surround and sash windows and rendered walls, beneath a recently replaced slate roof. In around 1900, it appears from an old photograph, to have had a 'Westmorland hood' (curved canopy, of which several examples can be seen in the locality), above the front door.

Westmorland House (the SPAR stores)

A splendid example of an elaborate Victorian iron shop front, which is a single storey extension built out from the main structure, a three-storey eighteenth century building. The wrought iron work consists of slender twisted columns, terminating in highly ornamental capitals. Five round arches link the columns. Above, the forward extension forms a balcony with decorative iron railings, the first floor has round-topped windows and a third storey is lit by earlier rectangular ones.

SPAR Stores.

Next comes the **Tufton Arms**, built in 1873, on the site of an earlier inn, the Crown and Mitre, by Sir Henry Tufton of Appleby Castle, a few years before the Shambles were removed and reflecting its age, when architecture drew heavily on the styles of earlier periods. Of pale grey dressed stone, the building is three storeys high, with numerous features combined to create a dominating presence in the lower market place. The roof of slate is complex, with several gables, that to the right of the entrance being half hipped and more prominent.

Looking at the facade, a verandah shelters the entrance, echoing the pentices which are a feature of many Westmorland barns. To the right, we find a buttress, supporting an oriel window (upstairs bay) emphasising the importance of the 'best' rooms. At the other end, a carriage way leads through to a cobbled yard and (originally) stabling. The hotel was, of course, built in the days when transport depended on horses. A shop (now a butcher's) is an integral part of the whole building.

Oriel window of the Tufton Arms, overlooking the market place.

More shops come next, across the narrow street from the Moot Hall. By looking up, you can see that the shop fronts have encroached into the market area, from the **eighteenth century building behind**, either side of a tall gabled extension. Below, the door of the eighteenth century building is visible.

Next, an arcade leads through an archway with a shop on each side, to a **Public Hall**. It was built by Sir Henry Tufton as an indoor market, a meeting hall and auditorium; in the twentieth century it also served as a cinema, a function recently revived.. The **Conservative Club**, also funded by Tufton, who had been ennobled as Lord Hothfield in 1882, and had changed his political allegiance from Liberal to Conservative, follows with more shops on the ground floor. The entrance has a curved pediment above it, a recessed balcony with the same motif over the door and a name plaque, under an arch. The central panel culminates in a gabled parapet complete with insignia carved in stone. Above each shop are tripartite windows on two storeys, those on the first floor with pediments and brackets, giving them emphasis. Photographic evidence shows the predecessors of these buildings and the Post Office. You can see them outside the front of Dent's newsagents.

The **Post Office** was rebuilt in 1912. Its style reflects the Edwardian period, but by looking up, you see the datestone of 1653, high in the new wall. Photographs show its predecessor, a thatched, single- storey house.

High Wiend comes after the Post Office, one of the ancient ways through to the back lane, between burgage plots.

18th century door.

Above the shops.

Conservative club and shops.

28, Boroughgate.

On the opposite corner of High Wiend, is a shop in a distinguished building, number **28, Boroughgate**. **Evidence of** its previous uses as a tea merchant's and apothecary's can be seen above the door. The cellar is entered at ground level in High Wiend. Notable features: walls of ashlar (smooth blocks of stone); stone quoins (corner stones); string course (raised line between floors); and six-pane sash windows to all three storeys. These windows have no 'horns' or lugs, (extensions to the sides of the upper sashes), indicating that they probably date from before the mid nineteenth century. Perhaps the most distinguishing feature is the stone canopy over the door. This is a Westmorland hood, several examples of which survive in the town and surrounding villages. These hoods consist of four pieces of stone which form a semi-circular shelter, on carved brackets. There is another example in Battlebarrow, across the Eden, and more are shown in old photographs at the newsagent's. A photograph of the Crown and Cushion over a hundred years ago shows that it had one of these, and the outline of it can still be seen.

From here to the top of Boroughgate, all the buildings keep to the same line and all are linked together, so that full use is made of the space available. Most have a passageway leading to the back of the building.

The Red House occupies a prominent position in Boroughgate. Spreading over several former burgage plots, it is perhaps the street's most imposing building. It was built in 1717, replacing an earlier house belonging to the Carleton family. Re-used stonework round the back of the house includes a dated door lintel (TC MC 1663). The building is of red sandstone under a Westmorland slate roof. Seven sash windows light the upper floor, six on the ground floor. The grand rooms are above a basement. 'Upstairs' and 'downstairs' are separated by a set of area steps leading down to a servants' entrance. A string course and change of stonework emphasise its distinction.

Thomas Carleton was agent for Lord Thanet of Appleby Castle, and the house was used as the judges' lodging when the Assize Court was held at the Castle. The main doorway, with bolection (convex) moulding and curved pediment, is approached up an imposing flight of steps, with nineteenth century iron railings. The whole building is high status and merits a Grade II* listing.

Classical House of 1717.

Moving up the street, the **Courtyard Gallery** is entered through the yard door, behind a late Georgian house. The Gallery is up a flight of steps in an outbuilding. Once used as a dame school, graffiti can be found around the walls of the courtyard, carved by former pupils. From the steps a good view of the back of the house can be obtained. Evidence of change over time is clear. The house front shows two sixteen-pane sash windows on each of the two floors.

The **White Hart** hotel (closed and converted to flats, now disused) is in contrast to the Red House, in having a rendered and painted front, with contrasting quoins. The three-storey building has sash windows on the upper two floors that don't align with the ground floor openings, suggesting that an earlier building was lower and heightened in the eighteenth century. The yard door is lower down the slope and would have led to the stable, which, according to an early nineteenth century description, when William Armathwaite was landlord, informs us that it had accommodation for ten horses. Other outbuildings included a slaughter house and butcher's shop, a malt kiln and a mule stable. In 1880, John Shaw turned it into a temperance hotel, in a period when abstinence from alcohol was fashionable. Notice the tethering rings for horses, either side of the main door.

36 Boroughgate (Grade II* listed), is formerly the **Black Bull** Inn. Built of red and buff sandstone, under a Westmorland slate roof, this exhibits the oldest plan form in the street. Called a cross passage plan, from the positioning of two doors leading through the house, behind the main hearth (look at the position of the chimney), the living space is entered by turning left past the back of the hearth, into a 'heck' (narrow passage beside the fireplace). This leads to a room with an inglenook. The dark corner near the fire was lit by a 'fire window', the small blocked rectangular window to the left of the door. This is just one of the clues to the development of the house that can be seen in the three-storey facade. You will see that one set of windows was seventeenth century and mullioned, but all are now blocked, the present windows dating from the 1800s. Modernisation of the frontage was chosen over rebuilding.

36, Boroughgate

Numbers 38 and 40, formerly the Butcher's Arms, have a stone ashlar front and end chimney stacks with a central passage to the rear and the main entrance to the left.

Numbers 42 and 44, formerly Rutland House and the Liberal Club, has the only carriage way to the rear on this side of the street. The passage divides the property into two equal halves, the right side now occupied by the Royal British Legion. Notice the cobbles down the centre of the passage, for the horses' hooves, while the flags on either side allowed cart wheels a smoother ride.

Numbers 42 and 44.

Passage for horse-drawn vehicles, cobbled centre with flags either side.

Number 48, Boroughgate.   *Ornamental Iron Porch.*

Number **48** is a complete late Georgian rebuilding, at least of the three-storey facade. Red sandstone, in regular blocks, all openings have plain painted surrounds. This is the only roof on the west side of the street with gable copings and 'kneelers' (the stone projections at the eaves, which support the coping stones).

Number **50**, lately known as Rose Cottage, is slightly older than its neighbour, described above. The projecting quoins and stuccoed front are painted. Over the main entrance is a rectangular fanlight, a feature of the houses at this end of the street. The only former gap between houses has been filled by building a small room over the passageway.

Numbers **52 to 58** were all refronted and/or rebuilt in the late eighteenth or early nineteenth centuries. They exhibit variations on a theme, having rectangular fanlights, sash windows, panelled doors, and either are rendered or show the sandstone. All have pretty gardens with iron railings.

The last building on Boroughgate's west side is **60 and 62**, and is unusual in being separate from the rest and end-on to the street, because of its position on the corner. The exterior is roughcast and the gable has sash windows, one lighting the attic space.

Like the Low Cross, the **High Cross** was paid for out of Lady Anne Clifford's bequest, replacing an earlier market boundary marker. Built c. 1680, with a Doric column on a plinth and a base of four stone steps, it was evidently a model for the Low Cross, erected a few years later. It became the location for the hiring of servants and labourers at the borough's long-established Whitsuntide Fair. The inscription facing down the street, 'Retain your Loyalty, Preserve your Rights', appears to be an eighteenth century addition, probably by the Tuftons, who inherited the Clifford wealth, alluding perhaps to an issue of local or national politics.

High Cross base with motto.

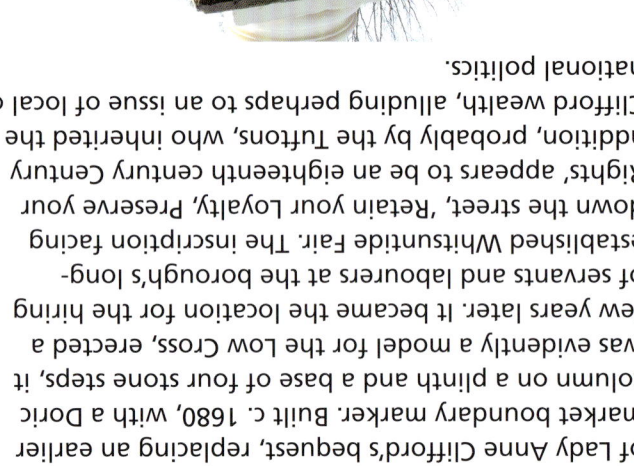

Iron lamp post.

Below it (on the north side) is an elegant double headed late nineteenth century iron lamp post which is also a listed structure. The lamps would have been powered by gas from the Appleby Gas Works at the end of Chapel Street. Electricity did not reach Appleby until 1934.

The 2 storey houses at **55-49 Boroughgate** are of late eighteenth or early nineteenth century date and form a pleasing group. They differ subtly but the overall effect is harmonious. Although they are quite elegant houses, they do not have front gardens. Houses on this side of the street also do not have access to a back lane, because the burgage plots finish at the River Eden.

The building material is red sandstone ashlar (finely dressed stone) with Westmorland or Welsh slate roofs. Nos 55 and 53 have stone coping on the gable ends. The front doors are panelled and no 51 has an impressive door case, with a dentilled pediment (triangular panel) above. The windows are all sashes without lugs, which shows that they are early. No 49 has plain stone door and window surrounds, and the masonry on that house is less finely dressed than the houses above.

Numbers 55 to 49.

View of St. Anne's hospital from the street.

St Anne's Hospital is an early example of a purpose-built almshouse which has survived relatively intact. It occupies 4 former burgage plots and was built1651-1653 by Lady Anne Clifford to house 12 sisters (inmates) and a mother (a resident warden). It is built as a cloister round a central courtyard, with a chapel in one corner. St Anne's is open 10 to 5 daily, and it is well worth stepping inside the cobbled courtyard. The coats of arms over the archway belong to Lady Anne and her mother, and the others round the yard represent Lady Anne's noble connections. The chapel is in lower left hand corner and retains some original seventeenth century fittings and wall paintings. You can also read Lady Anne's rules, which were strict! The accommodation for each sister was originally a single ground floor room, but this was altered in the nineteenth century to provide upstairs bedrooms. Note how the roof line slopes down the hill.

The courtyard with central garden, surrounded by cottages.

Another view of the courtyard, with the chapel door in the corner.

45-37 Boroughgate.

The 2-storey cottages at **45-37 Boroughgate** have all been rebuilt at various times and their features reflect that. They are built of squared coursed rubble, in contrast to the higher quality ashlar you saw in the row at the top of Boroughgate, and the door and window surrounds are plain. The ground rises uphill but the eaves are level, which means that no 45 has lower ceilings. What you see today is mainly eighteenth century but the stone-flagged passageway between nos 37 and 39 looks earlier.

Masonic hall.

The **Masonic Hall** (formerly Bank House) is a substantial early nineteenth century house, which has 3 storeys and a cellar. It is rendered with stone quoins (corner stones). It has sash windows, with plat bands (flat, horizontal mouldings) between storeys. The doorway was modified when it was converted from a private house into the Masonic Hall, and the ground floor windows appear to have been altered. See if you can spot the old name Bank House, which comes from its position on the hill with the river Eden to the rear: it was never a bank.

White Rails.

31 Boroughgate, formerly the Mechanics Institute

This building with its fancy bargeboards and Gothic revival windows looks as if it should be part of a railway station, but it was built as a Mechanics Institute. The Institute was founded in 1848, and as the date stone records, this building dates from 1851. By 1894, according to Kelly's Directory, it had "a library of over 2000 volumes and a reading room supplied with daily and weekly papers and magazines". In 1921 it housed a Labour Exchange. The building material is pale sandstone and unusually the building has no front door. The entrance is from the arched carriageway leading to the yard behind the former A'board Inn next door Note the clusters of diagonal chimneys.

White Rails is the only house on the east side of Boroughgate to have a front garden. It is an L-shaped mid eighteenth century house, and the position of the house in the plot creates room for a small garden. It is built of red sandstone ashlar with a moulded cornice (the projecting feature at the top of the walls). It has an elegant rectangular fanlight above the door (as at no 50 on the other side of Boroughgate) and a driveway at the side leading to a coach house.

31 Boroughgate.

The **White House** is Appleby's most individually memorable building. It is a fine, substantial eighteenth century mansion and would have been the height of elegance when it was remodelled in the 1750s and 1760s in the early Strawberry Hill Gothic style, for John Robinson, Sir James Lowther's agent and man of business, who became an MP, first for Westmorland, then Harwich, and was Treasury Secretary from 1770 to 1782, with a reputation as a political fixer.

The building is whitewashed, with a hipped Westmorland slate roof. It has a stone plinth, alternating quoins and three squared stone string courses dividing the floors. The original entrance would have been from the street elevation, but as part of the remodelling an elaborate side entrance was created. The windows all have similar surrounds with ogee window heads (double curved) and traceried sashes. There is also a similar window in the wall of the former inn next door. The building has 3 storeys, a cellar and an attic. If you look up at the roof, you can see ocular (oval) attic lights.

Exterior of the White House.

Window detail of the White House.

23 Boroughgate, is a fine three-storey house built of red sandstone ashlar dating back to the late eighteenth century. It has been a greengrocer's shop for over a century. In 1921, according to Kelly's Directory, it was occupied by Frederick Stephenson, nurseryman and fruiterer. It has an attractive Victorian shop front. An archway leads to Court 2 behind it, and the entrance to cellar is from the street, taking advantage of the steep slope.

21 Boroughgate, former Midland Bank, originally the Cumberland Union Banking Co Ltd, later Martin's Bank, now Low Howgill shop.

19 Boroughgate, former Barclay's Bank, originally the Carlisle and Cumberland Bank (1876), now apartments.

These rival banks were built next door to one another, and appear to be competing with their architecture as well as for customers. Originally the bank managers lived on the premises. The stone is very different from the other buildings nearby. No 21 is high quality ashlar and no 19 is stone with ashlar dressings Both buildings have fancy parapets and elaborate wrought iron balconies, and they also have marble columns and elegant capitals on the ground floor windows to impress customers. The entrances face away from each other and no 21 has an arch to the rear yard.